ACKNOWLEDGEMENTS

Thank you to the wonderful neurodivergent individuals and professionals who reviewed this workbook and provided edits and feedback. And an extra big thank you to Mikayla, an inspiring young Autistic adult who provided hours and hours of impeccable editing and tips - I couldn't have finished this without you.

CONTENTS

1   About This Workbook
2   DBT Skills

3   Section 1: Everyday Well-being

4   Self-care
6   A guide to my needs
7   Support and accommodations
10 Personal crisis plan
11 Creating a sensory-friendly safe space
12 Affirmations for neurodivergent folks
13 Affirmations for RSD

15 Section 2: Mindfulness

16 Mindfulness
18 The wise mind
22 Identify your values
25 Mindful appreciation
26 Self check-In
28 Observing with your senses
29 Accessible mindfulness exercises
33 Mindfulness with pets

35 Section 3: Distress Tolerance

36 Distress tolerance/STOP
37 Mammalian diving reflex
39 TIPP skill
40 Meltdowns
44 Sensory self-soothing
46 IMPROVE the environment
48 A list of stims
49 Special interests

51 Section 4: Emotional Regulation

52 The role of emotions
54 Emotional responses
55 Alexithymia
56 Describing your emotions
59 The Window of Tolerance
61 Emotional regulation
62 Check the facts
64 Act Intentionally

67 Section 5: Managing Sensory Needs

68 Sensory profile and needs
69 Hypersensitivity
71 Hyposensitivity
73 Sensory overload
74 My sensory profile
76 Build a sensory toolkit

ABOUT THIS WORKBOOK

Hi, I'm Sonny Jane and my pronouns are they/them. It's wonderful to meet you! I'm multiply neurodivergent - or more specifically, I'm an Autistic ADHDer living with Bipolar and in recovery with Borderline Personality Disorder. I'm also a lived experience educator, consultant and advocate who's passionate about neurodiversity and supporting neurodivergent individuals.

As neurodivergent individuals, we can express different types of distress from living in a society that isn't designed for our differences. It isn't just emotional distress but also meltdowns and sensory distress that we can experience too. One of the best things we can do to support ourselves is to figure out ways to manage our distress, and Dialectical Behavioural Therapy (DBT) skills are just one way to do this.

Dialectical Behaviour Therapy was founded by Dr Marsha Lineham for individuals living with Borderline Personality Disorder. DBT focuses on four components; mindfulness, interpersonal effectiveness, distress tolerance and emotional regulation. However, in order to remain neurodivergent friendly, interpersonal effectiveness has been removed. Instead, there's a whole section on our sensory needs and distress tolerance now includes information on and tools on managing meltdowns.

While DBT skills can be valuable and helpful, they don't always meet the needs of neurodivergent individuals - especially Autistic and ADHD individuals. That's why I created this workbook, a way for neurodivergent folks to learn DBT skills in a way that works for you, at your own pace.

I want to reiterate that DBT does not focus on compliance or changing who we are. It's about giving us the skills to identify as well as regulate our emotions, find ways to manage our distress and both recognise, fulfil and advocate for our needs.

This workbook is not a substitute for counselling, therapy or any other mental health service.

DBT SKILLS

This is a self-guided workbook aimed to take you through skills based on three areas: mindfulness, distress tolerance, emotional regulation and sensory needs. The chapters can be read in any order and you are welcome to skip any skills if you like. There is a strong focus on choice, always choice. In addition, interpersonal effectiveness has intentionally been left out, and there's now parts addressing sensory needs and managing meltdowns.

MINDFULNESS	Skills to help you ground yourself, create awareness & focus on the present.
DISTRESS TOLERANCE	Skills and tools to help you manage moments of distress, overwhelm and overload.
EMOTIONAL REGULATION	Skills to help you understand, manage and respond to your emotions.

So, how can you determine what skill you should use?

I've created a little guide to help you choose a skill that matches the intensity of your emotion. Remember, everyone is different so this is only a suggestion!

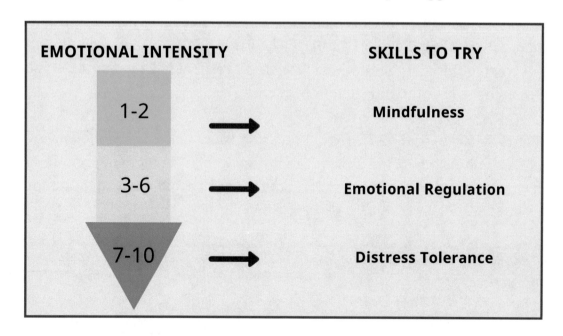

EMOTIONAL INTENSITY	SKILLS TO TRY
1-2	**Mindfulness**
3-6	**Emotional Regulation**
7-10	**Distress Tolerance**

SECTION 1:

EVERYDAY WELL-BEING

4   Self-care

6   A guide to my needs

7   Support and accommodations

10 Personal crisis plan

11 Creating a sensory-friendly safe space

12 Affirmations for neurodivergent folks

13 Affirmations for rejection sensitive dysphoria

DOODLE HERE

SELF-CARE

Self-care is an important part of looking after our well-being and helps prevent us from reaching points of distress. In addition, it can be helpful to practice self-care as learning new skills can be exhausting and even frustrating.

Self-care is all about meeting our needs, and these needs include physical, emotional, social and sensory needs. Everyone has different needs, but to get you started, here are some examples of what those needs can look like:

PHYSICAL

taking your meds
getting enough sleep
having breaks
drinking enough water
stretching or movement

EMOTIONAL

therapy
expressing boundaries
getting affection
things that make you feel good
special interests

SOCIAL

visiting friends
date nights
spending time alone
curating social media
boundaries

SENSORY

having sensory breaks
wearing comfy clothing
avoiding busy places
using sunglasses or earplugs
stimming

Everyone is different with different needs, so you might even find that you need to practice self-care more in one area than another and that's okay! On the next page, there's space for you to figure out what you can do to meet your needs every day.

If you struggle asking for support or you have a difficult time expressing what you need, I've introduced a handy worksheet called 'a guide to my needs' that you can share with a friend, partner, caregiver or even a housemate whenever you need support.

REGULAR SELF-CARE

In this space, you can list the things you can do on a regular basis to meet your self-care needs. Everyone is different so you might even find that you need to practice self-care more in one area than another.

PHYSICAL

EMOTIONAL

SOCIAL

SENSORY

A GUIDE TO MY NEEDS

If you struggle with asking for support or you have a difficult time expressing what you need, you can use this to communicate or share with a friend, partner, caregiver or even a housemate whenever you need support.

I NEED YOUR HELP WHEN...

I WILL ASK FOR HELP BY...

YOU CAN HELP ME BY...

I WOULD LIKE TO HEAR...

SUPPORT & ACCOMMODATIONS

If we don't look after our everyday well-being, it becomes harder to regulate our emotions and we're more likely to reach a point of distress. We need to normalise asking for support and accomodations as a way of looking after our well-being. Using this wheel model, we can communicate to the people around us which areas of life we might need support and accomodations in.

SLEEP

falling asleep
staying asleep
sleep schedules
nightmares

WORK/STUDY

due dates
instructions
flexibility
uniforms

COMMUNICATION

phone calls
appointments
advocacy
non-verbal

DAILY LIVING

cleaning
organisation
hygiene
reminders

SENSORY

home
meltdowns
clothing
accomodations

FINANCES

costs of aids
debt
impulsivity
tracking/planning

EATING/COOKING

sensory
intolerances
executive function
going shopping

RELATIONSHIPS

social rules
stigma
communication
boundaries

SUPPORT & ACCOMMODATIONS

This is an example of the different areas where someone may need support and accomodations.

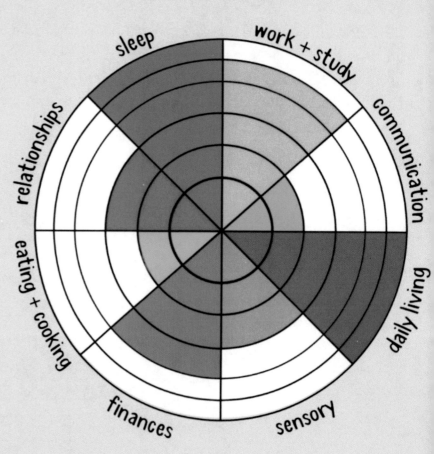

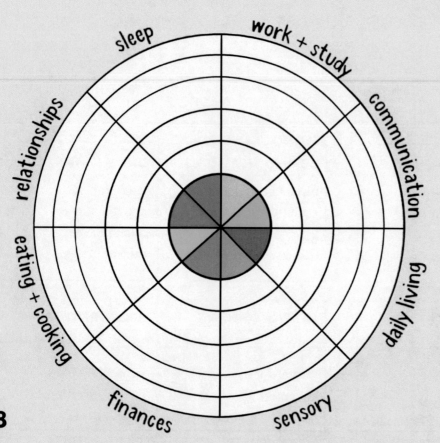

FILL IN AREAS WHERE YOUR SKILLS AND STRENGTHS ARE

1 - I need to work on some skills

2 - I'm developing skills/strengths

3 - I've got a few skills in this area

4 - I can name at least four

5 - I'm nailing this area

SUPPORT & ACCOMMODATIONS

FILL IN THE AREAS OF YOUR LIFE THAT ARE IMPACTED THE MOST

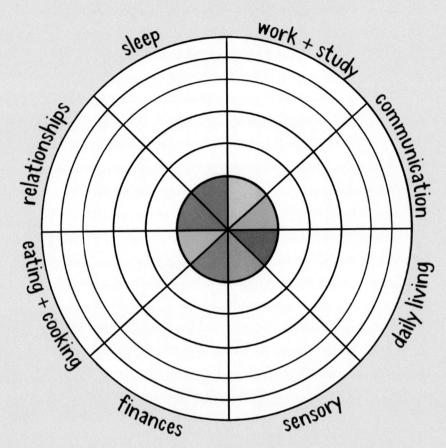

1 - No impact on my quality of life
2 - Occasionally but minimal impact
3 - Sometimes but easy to manage
4 - Regularly interferes
5 - Uses up all my spoons

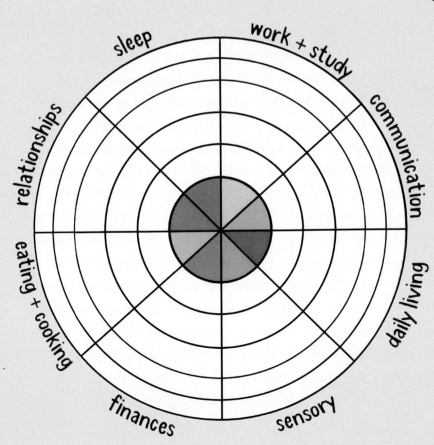

FILL IN AREAS OF YOUR LIFE WHERE YOU NEED THE MOST SUPPORT

1 - I need minimal support
2 - I need support occasionally
3 - I need support day to day
4 - A carer would be nice
5 - Just do it for me, thanks

PERSONAL CRISIS PLAN

Sometimes it helps to have a personal crisis plan ready to go especially as we might have a harder time remembering the important and basic things during a crisis or times of high stress. You can use this plan as a reminder whenever you've reached a point of distress.

I KNOW I'M TRIGGERED OR IN NEED OF SUPPORT WHEN:

THREE WAYS I CAN DISTRACT MYSELF ARE:

SAFE PEOPLE I CAN CALL OR MESSAGE:

NAME: _____   _____   _____

CONTACT DETAILS: _____   _____   _____

COPING TOOLS OR SKILLS THAT HELP ARE:

CREATING A SENSORY SAFE SPACE

An neurodivergent individuals, our sensory needs are an important part of managing our every day well-being. One way we can take care of our well-being is by having a sensory safe space we can escape to in times of need.

FIND YOUR SPACE:

You might not have access to turning an entire room into a sensory safe space but there are other options you can try like finding a corner of your room, under the stairs or by setting up a little tent indoors.

CHOOSE YOUR LIGHTING:

Try and think about what kind of colours or lighting is most comforting for you. I tend to go for purple, blue and white lights. Many people prefer a "warm white" rather than a "cool white". You can hang up fairy lights, use a galaxy projector light, or find some cool lamps.

WHERE TO SIT:

When it comes to the perfect seating for your sensory safe space, it's good to think about what kind of sensory input you need in the moment. Would you feel more comfortable on a bean bag wrapped up in a blanket, swinging in a chair, or bouncing on an exercise ball? Include a few, give yourself choice!

WHAT TO PUT IN IT:

This is the fun part; filling up your sensory safe space with sensory-friendly items and all your favourite things! Here is a little list to get you started:

fidget items
weighted blanket
sensory tray
ear plugs/headphones

chewellery
favourite pictures and affirmations
soothing music and sound machine
puzzles, slime or putty

AFFIRMATIONS FOR NEURODIVERGENT FOLKS

It can be difficult being neurodivergent in a neurotypical world and as a result, we can often hear and internalise some negative views, beliefs and stereotypes. These affirmations are neurodivergent friendly and I hope they will bring you some comfort.

It's okay if most strategies and tools that were designed for and by neurotypical people don't work for me.

My brain works exactly the way it was designed to, and I deserve to find ways to support my brain.

I will not hide my identity and neurodivergent traits just because they make people uncomfortable.

I can forget to close cabinets, brush my teeth, and reply to messages and still be worthy.

I do not have to hold myself to neurotypical standards, rules, or expectations.

My sensory differences are real and valid, and they deserve to be accommodated.

AFFIRMATIONS FOR REJECTION SENSITIVE DYSPHORIA

Rejection Sensitive Dysphoria is a sensitivity to rejection and criticism that is a common experience for neurodivergent individuals, especially ADHDers. RSD causes an intense emotional response that reinforces messages to us that we aren't good enough or no-one likes us. This is why I've included some affirmations to combat these messages below:

My interests are valid, and I am allowed to be excited and passionate about them even if other people aren't.

People disagreeing with me does not mean my lived experience or my opinion are invalid.

I am allowed to ask for reassurance and I am worthy of people's time and attention.

I am allowed to ask questions and require certain pty in order to feel safety and control.

Some people won't like me no matter what and that is not a reflection of how likeable I am.

I decide what thoughts to reject and let pass.

WRITE YOUR OWN AFFIRMATIONS

You can write and add your own affirmations here. You can come back to this list when you need to remind yourself or whenever you might need comfort. Maybe you can even share this list with a partner or a friend so they can say these things to you in times of need:

SECTION 2: MINDFULNESS

16   Mindfulness

18   The Wise mind

20   Finding and engaging your wise mind

22   Your values

25   Mindful appreciation

26   Self check-in

28   Observing with your senses

29   Accessible mindfulness exercises

33   Mindfulness with pets

DOODLE HERE

MINDFULNESS

Mindfulness is a foundational skill within DBT and is often seen as being necessary to utilise emotional regulation and distress tolerance skills. To put simply, mindfulness is the ability to be present in the moment where we are aware of what's happening within us and outside of us. Most importantly, we do this without judgement.

If it sounds difficult, that's because it really can be - especially if you're someone who might already struggle with attention or interoception. Some mindfulness practices, such as visualising and breathing-based mindfulness, may also be uncomfortable or difficult for some people.

That's why it's important to remember (and celebrate!) that everyone responds to mindfulness differently.

Some neurodivergent individuals, especially autistic folks, may experience aphantasia, an inability to visualise something in one's mind. For these folks, mindfulness exercises that rely on visualisation aren't really effective.

This is why in this workbook, you'll find exercises that explore mindfulness in other ways besides breathing and visualisation.

What can mindfulness help with?

focusing and paying attention.	allowing intrusive or judgemental thoughts to pass.
identifying your needs.	making intentional choices and decisions.
recognising when you're reaching sensory overload.	coping with rejection and criticism.
increasing self-awareness.	practicing compassion.
regulating emotions.	

WHEN TO USE MINDFULNESS

When practicing mindfulness, here's some things to remember:

You don't have to try all these skills at once. Try practising one skill at a time.

Do not judge yourself: let any thoughts, emotions or sensations pass with compassion and an open mind.

It's okay if you find your attention drifting, try and guide yourself back or perhaps incorporate stimming into your mindfulness activity.

You don't need to close your eyes, you can just stare at a spot on the ground if that feels more natural/comfortable.

There's actually no right or wrong way to be mindful - it's important to figure out what works for you like focusing on an external object or selecting movement based activities.

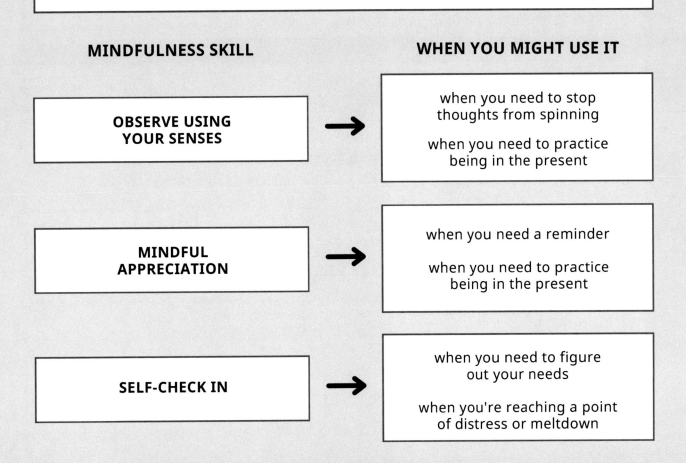

MINDFULNESS SKILL	WHEN YOU MIGHT USE IT
OBSERVE USING YOUR SENSES →	when you need to stop thoughts from spinning when you need to practice being in the present
MINDFUL APPRECIATION →	when you need a reminder when you need to practice being in the present
SELF-CHECK IN →	when you need to figure out your needs when you're reaching a point of distress or meltdown

Use the following skills and tools in the rest of this section to explore and practice mindfulness.

THE WISE MIND

In DBT, there are three states of mind. These are described as: the logical mind, the emotional mind and the wise mind. The goal of our wise mind is to take the best of both worlds from our logical mind and our emotional mind to define what our wise mind means to us as individuals. We all have our own unique wise mind.

Often, for whatever reason, we can get stuck in our logical mind or emotional mind and while there are strengths and benefits to both, there are also some difficulties that occur when we remain in either mind.

Logical Mind:

A state of mind that is based on facts, reason and logic. In the logical mind, emotions are not taken into consideration. When using your logical mind, you might be looking at things analytically.

Might be good for: planning, researching, making decisions, analysing, control, grounding, learning skills.

Emotional mind:

A state of mind during which your emotions influence your behaviour and thoughts. In the emotional mind, it can be hard to access the logical mind and think clearly. If you're in an emotional mind, you may act impulsively and intensely.

Might be good for: passion, motivation, creativity, empathy, adapting, relationships, communication.

Wise mind:

A state of mind that's a combination of both the logical mind and emotional mind. We all have our own wise mind. In the wise mind, we respect and listen to both our emotional and logical mind.

Might be good for: communicating, making decisions, responding to events/situations, relationships, balance.

THE WISE MIND

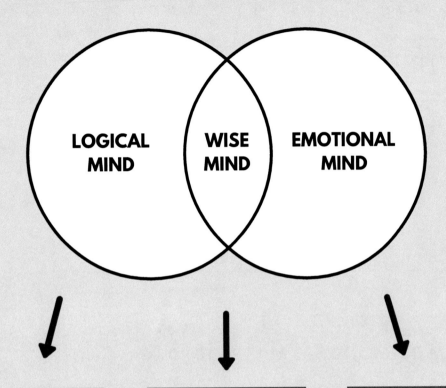

CAUTIOUS	THE MIDDLE PATH	IMPULSIVE
ANALYTICAL	INNER WISDOM	CREATIVE
LOGICAL	RULED BY:	PASSIONATE
FACTUAL	- CHOICE	MOOD-DEPENDENT
RULED BY:	- FACTS	RULED BY:
- FACTS	- REASON	- URGES
- LOGIC	- VALUES,	- FEELINGS
- CONTROL	- EMOTION	- EMOTIONS
	MY WISE MIND FEELS AND LOOKS LIKE:	

FINDING YOUR WISE MIND

Use this space to describe your logical mind, emotional mind and wise mind.

WHEN I AM IN LOGICAL MIND, I TEND TO...

WHEN I AM IN EMOTIONAL MIND, I TEND TO...

WHEN I AM IN WISE MIND, I TEND TO...

ENGAGING THE WISE MIND

Below are some strategies you can use to practice engaging your wise mind.

MINDFULNESS

Notice your feelings, reactions, thoughts and any sensations happening in your body. Observe what is happening without any judgement or criticism.

CURIOSITY

Investigate what is happening with curiousity & compassion. Ask yourself: "What is this reaction trying to tell me?" and "What do I need right now?"

COMPASSION

Practice being compassionate, caring and understanding with yourself, just like you would a friend. You can even have a conversation with yourself out loud.

CONSIDER YOUR VALUES

One way to engage the wise mind is to remind yourself of your values. Does the action, behaviour or choice align with a value?

IDENTIFY YOUR VALUES

Values can be described as your morals, ethics, principles or what you value in life and how you aspire to live. Values can also be described as something that gives your life meaning and importance while helping you to define your priorities.

Everyone has different values and discovering your values can be helpful in stressful situations such as work, studying or relationships because it can help guide your choices and actions.

Knowing and remembering your values can help you with making choices, tolerating stressful situations as well as responding to your needs accordingly.

Some questions to help you identify what's important to you might be:

- when were you happiest? what were you doing?
- when were you most proud?
- when have you been most satisfied and fulfilled?
- what are your special interests?
- what do you feel strongly about?
- have there been times you have stood up for something?

Below are some examples of different values that you can explore. See if you identify with some of them or any of them. You can also add your own.

connection	authenticity	adventure
pleasure	creativity	compassion
courage	honesty	security
wisdom	passion	learning
strength	empathy	humour
freedom	fairness	kindness

IDENTIFY YOUR VALUES

It might be helpful to identify what your values look like. It's okay if you value different things in different areas of your life!

MY SOCIAL VALUES

MY PERSONAL VALUES

MY POLITICAL VALUES

MY WORK VALUES

VALUE ACTION PLAN

What can you do to prioritise your values in your life? These actions come be small everyday things or things you might want to remember to do more of in your life.

IDENTIFY YOUR VALUE

IDENTIFY SOME ACTIONS THAT ALIGN WITH YOUR VALUE

IDENTIFY YOUR VALUE

IDENTIFY SOME ACTIONS THAT ALIGN WITH YOUR VALUE

IDENTIFY YOUR VALUE

IDENTIFY SOME ACTIONS THAT ALIGN WITH YOUR VALUE

24

MINDFUL APPRECIATION

Sometimes it can be really difficult remembering the good things in your life especially when as neurodivergent individuals, we might struggle with permanence or emotion flooding. This is why I've included some prompts to help you remember some things that bring you joy or comfort - neurodivergent style!

CURRENT SPECIAL INTERESTS OR HYPERFIXATIONS

YOUR FAVOURITE SENSORY OR FIDGET ITEMS

YOUR FAVOURITE WAYS TO STIM

PEOPLE WHO HAVE MADE YOU HAPPY LATELY

SELF CHECK-IN

Checking in with ourselves is probably the most helpful thing we can do every day. When we do this, we can figure out what our needs are in the moment and use that information to respond to our needs and take care of ourselves.

You can use this skill to check in with your basic needs like making sure you've had some water or eaten food. You can also use this skill to determine whether you need a sensory break or support.

You can use the prompts below to guide your self check-in.

WHAT EMOTIONS AM I FEELING RIGHT NOW?

WHAT ARE THESE FEELINGS TRYING TO TELL ME?

HOW IS MY BODY REACTING?

WHAT AM I THINKING RIGHT NOW?

HOW IS MY MOOD?
- how am I feeling?
- are my emotions fleeting or long lasting?

HOW IS MY ENERGY?
- am I tired, energetic or average?
- do I need to eat something or rest?

HOW IS MY BREATHING?
- am I breathing fast or slow?
- am I exhaling from my stomach or chest?

HOW IS MY FOCUS?
- am I able to concentrate or am I distracted?
- am I able to focus for a long or short time?

HOW IS MY BODY DOING?
- do I have any tension or pain?
- do I need to rest my body?

WHAT NEXT?

WRITE YOUR OWN

How is my mood?

- emotional regulation
- have a nap
- take a break
- talk to a friend

How is my energy?

- eat something
- have a nap
- drink water
- sensory output

How is my breathing?

- practice mindfulness
- stim
- use senses to soothe
- breathing exercises

How is my focus?

- have a break
- use a fidget toy
- change of scenery
- make it a game

How is my body?

- take your meds
- have a nap
- stim
- stretch

My sensory needs?

- dim the lighting
- turn off sounds
- stim away
- do heavy work for input

27

OBSERVING WITH YOUR SENSES

Here are some ideas to get you started observing using your senses, with room to add your own.

OBSERVE WITH YOUR EYES

Go for a walk in a park and observe the birds and nature.

Find an object in your room or backyard and observe the details.

Lay on the ground watching the clouds float by.

Set up a light projector and focus on the moving lights.

_____

OBSERVE USING TASTE

Suck on a lollipop or hard candy and observe the flavours. Bonus if it has layers!

Drink a cup of tea and observe the flavours and temperature

_____

_____

_____

_____

OBSERVE USING SOUND

Listen to music and observe each note and instrument.

Take a walk and listen to the sounds of nature.

Put on white noise, waves, or whale music.

_____

_____

_____

OBSERVE USING SMELL

Light some candles and breathe in, noticing the scent.

Take a walk, focusing on the scents of nature.

As you cook a meal, focus on the smell of the ingredients.

_____

_____

_____

ACCESSIBLE MINDFULNESS EXERCISES

It's really important to acknowledge and even celebrate the fact that everyone has a different brain and everyone responds to mindfulness differently.

Some individuals may find visualising and breathing-based mindfulness practices difficult or uncomfortable, which means certain mindfulness practices may not work for them. Some individuals may struggle to focus on internal sensations like breathing or body checks and that's okay too.

Remember, just because certain practices don't work for you doesn't mean you're doing it wrong - it just means it doesn't work for you and you need to find different techniques that do work for you. As you explore these practices, remember to be gentle and check in with yourself. Ask yourself how your body is responding. Ask yourself what feelings come up before, during or after these practices.

USE YOUR ENVIRONMENT

If you find yourself being pulled into your inner thoughts and sensations when using mindfulness, use your environment to ground yourself.

Focus on your surroundings by naming objects like the books on your shelf, the patterns in the rug, the number of tiles in the bathroom. If it helps, try naming the objects out loud or focusing on the details.

MINDFULLY LISTEN TO MUSIC

Tuning into ourselves and sitting in silence can be uncomfortable or even triggering for some people. Mindfully listening to music can be a way to direct your attention from your internal experience to something outside yourself like music.

Pay attention to what you're hearing; listen to the layers of the music, the complexities, the sounds of each instrument.

ACCESSIBLE MINDFULNESS EXERCISES

SOUND OF YOUR BREATH

Hold your hand in front of your mouth and exhale so you can hear the sound of your breath. Continue exhaling and inhaling while maintaining the sound.

Concentrate on the *sound* of your breathing, rather than counting your breathing, letting the sounds be your anchor.

COMPARE TWO

Find two objects that are similar like a pair of shoes, a couple of pillows, two mugs on your coffee table or a pair of candles next to each other.

Focus on noticing the differences of both objects: the shape and height, the texture, the colour and the small details of each object.

VISUAL STIMMING

Trace patterns in the environment around you with your finger, or your eyes, like the cracks in the ceiling or the patterns in the rug.

Alternatively, choose a word or even a sentence and trace the word in front of you, focusing on the way your finger moves through the air.

ACCESSIBLE MINDFULNESS EXERCISES

EXPLORE WITH PLAY-DOH, CLAY OR PLASTICINE

Explore the modelling material with your hands and notice the texture, the smell and the colour.

Experience it free from any expectation.

As you knead the material with your hands, focus on any changes and how those changes feel. Roll it into a ball or flatten it with your hand.

MINDFUL EATING

Pick a fruit which you can peel with your hands, like a banana, an orange, or my favourite - a mandarin. As you peel it, notice the texture and what the layer reveals underneath.

Notice the taste, texture, smell, colours and temperature with each bite.

MINDFUL STIMMING

Did you know that stimming can help us to focus and ground ourselves, as well as help us to regulate?

Sometimes, freeing the stim is the perfect way to create harmony and calm within us and bring us into the present moment. Try stim dancing or using some fidget items.

ACCESSIBLE MINDFULNESS EXERCISES

FIND A PERSONAL ANCHOR

Breathing is often a common anchor in mindfulness practices but when we can't trust or use our breathing, we can use a physical anchor like an object. Find an anchor that works for you; you might find that it's a personal object or a sensory object.

Sit with the anchor and explore it with whatever senses you prefer; use the anchor to practice mindfulness and ground yourself to the present moment.

HELPFUL PROMPTS

- What are your eyes or hands drawn to first?

- How does the object feel in your hand?
Focus on the weight of the object...

- Is the object stationary or is it moving around?

What does the surface of the object or item look like?
Focus on the texture... Shiny? Dull? Multi-textured?

- Does the surface have one colour or multiple colours?
Try looking at it in a different light or from a different angle...

- Does the object have round or sharp corners?

- Does the object have multiple surfaces?
Notice how they all connect...

- Can you feel the difference in the surfaces and textures?

- Is the object rigid or is it bendable?

- What do you notice that's unique about it?

MINDFULNESS WITH PETS

OBSERVE YOUR PET

Observe your pet and the way your pet looks at you or the way they make you feel. What do you notice about your pet?

Describe the way your pet looks by focusing on the texture of their fur, feathers or scales. Focus on the way their coat feels.

Participate by staying in the moment with your pet - perhaps talk to your pet or try cuddling them to stay present.

YOUR SENSES WITH YOUR PET

You probably do this already if you have a soft and cuddly friend, but when you're upset, you can hold them or cuddle them, use your senses to focus on the way they feel, the way they sound when they purr and the way they smell, especially if you bury your face in their fur.

...Maybe don't taste your pet ;)

ACTIVITIES WITH YOUR PET

Sometimes we might find it easier to be mindful while we're doing an activity; I know I do! You can do an activity or two with your pet/s!

Do an activity with your pet - washing them, grooming them or taking your pet for a walk. As you do so, focus on remaining present in the activity with your pet.

MINDFULNESS SUMMARY

What mindfulness practices are most helpful for you?

What are some signs that you need to use these skills?

Can you identify any barriers or accommodations needed in using these skills?

What reminders do you need to use these mindfulness tools?

SECTION 3:

DISTRESS TOLERANCE

36   Distress tolerance/STOP

37   Mammalian diving reflex

39   TIPP skill

40   Meltdowns

44   Sensory self-soothing

46   IMPROVE the environment

48   A list of stims

49   Special interests

DOODLE HERE

DISTRESS TOLERANCE

Distress tolerance is about managing stress and distress to keep it at a manageable level/level we can cope with. As neurodivergent individuals who are likely to experience high levels of stress living in a neurotypical society, these skills can be helpful and important.

As neurodivergent individuals, we're likely to experience distress when we're experiencing sensory overload, when we're experiencing Rejection Sensitivity from our RSD, when we're struggling to regulate our emotions, or when we're close to meltdown.

These skills can help us manage and tolerate distress, but distress tolerance should always come from a place of listening to what we need and responding accordingly.

Distress tolerance skills can be utilised when you are:

- overwhelmed by stressors like multiple tasks.
- feeling the urge to act on negative emotions.
- feeling overwhelmed and you can't think clearly.
- experiencing emotional or sensory overload.
- close to a meltdown.

When you're feeling overwhelmed or distressed, you can remember STOP so you can proceed mindfully and intentionally.

S STOP, PAUSE, AND DON'T REACT

T TAKE A STEP BACK, WALK AWAY AND TAKE A DEEP BREATH

O OBSERVE - NOTICE YOUR SURROUNDINGS AND HOW YOU FEEL

P PROCEED MINDFULLY - WHAT CAN YOU DO?

MAMMALIAN DIVING REFLEX

Have you ever wondered why splashing cold water on your face calms you down?

Using the mammalian diving reflex is my favourite tool in my coping toolbox. If you've ever wondered why breathing exercises help anxiety or why splashing your face with cold water feels calming, this is actually why - our mammalian diving reflex!

We all have the mammalian diving reflex - it's an innate physiological response that activates when you're submerged in freezing water, and it's why mammals like whales and dolphins can survive in the deep ocean. It's a survival mechanism, basically.

When we experience anxiety, panic or distress, our body goes into "fight or flight" mode. In this state, our heart starts racing, we might struggle to control our breathing, and we might even get an odd feeling in our limbs.

This makes things even more distressing which is why utilising the mammalian diving reflex is my first go-to because it can help us to lower these responses by using an innate physiological response. Super handy, hey?

The mammalian reflex activates the parasympathetic nervous system that creates or mimics relaxation and as a result, you get immediate relief because your heart rate slows down, your breathing slows down and as the blood flows away from your limbs, you'll start sweating less and your muscles will relax.

You can't go diving every time you're feeling overwhelmed, but (as long as you have access to something cold) you CAN activate this reflex whenever you need to.

IMPORTANT REMINDERS

In order for this skill to work, you need to ensure the area around your cheeks and above your eyes receive the input from the water.

If you have blood pressure or heart problems, please speak to your medical professional before trying this skill.

Adapted from Linehan, M. (June 6-7, 2011). Updates to emotion regulation and crisis survival skills in dialectical behavior therapy. Austin, TX: Behavior Tech, LLC.

MAMMALIAN DIVING REFLEX

METHOD ONE

Fill a bowl or a sink with cold water that is ice cold - water from the tap with some ice cubes works a treat.

In order to do this, you'll need to bend over so make sure you are comfortable, sit down if you need.

Hold your breath and submerge your face into the cold water for as long as is safe for you - try for 30 seconds.

As you can sit back up and open your eyes, notice your heart rate and your breathing start to slow down.

METHOD TWO

I tend to prefer this method because it's a lot more simple and quicker to do especially when I'm in a panic.

Keep a soft ice pack in the freezer for times like this.

Once you have the soft ice pack or even a bag of frozen peas, you want to make sure you're sitting so you can lean forward.

Cover your eyes with the ice pack, lean forward and hold your breath as you count to 20 or 30 seconds in your mind.

As you lean back and remove the ice pack from your face, breathe out slowly and notice as your heart rate slows down.

Remember, you need to hold your breath as if you were truly diving for it to activate the reflex. The longer you can hold your breath (safely), the better the results.

TIPP SKILL

The TIPP acronym is a great skill for moments of distress, panic or when you're feeling overwhelmed. This skill can help provide you with relief from the physiological effects of distress or emotions so you can think more clearly, process information and utilise other skills.

You can start by trying one of these and seeing what works:

TEMPERATURE
(to calm down immediately)

- use an ice pack or something frozen
- lean over and hold your breath
- hold for 30 seconds

INTENSE EXERCISE
(to calm your body down)

- engage in intense exercise for a short period of time
- expend your body's stored up energy
- stim dancing is a great way!

PACED BREATHING
(slow down your breathing)

- breathe in for four seconds, hold for four, breathe out for four
- figure out what pace works for you (3, 5, 7 works too!)

PAIRED MUSCLE RELAXATION
(to help relax your body)

- work on one section of your body at a time
- while breathing in, tense your muscles
- while breathing out, relax your muscles

MANAGING MELTDOWNS

Meltdowns are an involuntary response that can occur in a time of crisis or distress where we often lose control of our behaviour and responses.

Meltdowns often happen when we become dysregulated or overstimulated by stress, sensory input, our emotions and more because our body and brain is communicating to us that we have reached (and surpassed) a limit.

While people might see the meltdown happen as a result of a single event or trigger, meltdowns are always due to ongoing combination of factors that lead up to the big show.

Remember, meltdowns are not tantrums.

Meltdowns can look like:

shouting and screaming throwing things crying or loss of verbal words self-injury like hitting your head rocking back and forth	shutting down inability to communicate pacing or escaping hyperventilating physically curling inwards

While meltdowns can lead to behaviours that may cause hurt, our behaviours are not intentional because we aren't in control. This is why it's important to hold compassion for yourself when a meltdown happens.

Meltdowns are also super tiring and emotionally draining, which is why taking care of ourselves afterwards is really important. I often feel like I have an "emotional headache", I've been drained of energy, and just need to lie in the dark.

Mapping out our meltdowns, triggers and warning signs can help us better respond to and manage our meltdowns as well as find ways to prevent or minimise them.

You can find a Meltdown Mapping worksheet on page 42.

MELTDOWN PREVENTION TIPS

listen to your body

create a routine that works for you

make a meltdown plan for loved ones to use

learn your triggers + create a plan

create a sensory toolbox with your favourite sensory items

regular sensory breaks

identify early warning signs

allow yourself space to unmask

use AAC or written communication

have an exit strategy for situations

give yourself time to stim

utilise noise cancelling headphones and sunglasses

plan for events and outings in advance

reduce triggers like sensory input asap

deep pressure like weighted blankets

MELTDOWN MAPPING

MELTDOWN TRIGGERS

EARLY WARNING SIGNS

COPING STRATEGIES THAT CAN BE PUT IN PLACE

YOUR NEEDS OR BOUNDARIES DURING A MELTDOWN

MELTDOWN RECOVERY IDEAS

MELTDOWN TIP SHEET
FILL THIS IN FOR LOVES ONES AND FAMILY

EARLY WARNING SIGNS TO PAY ATTENTION TO:

PLEASE DO THESE THINGS WHEN YOU NOTICE THE WARNING SIGNS:

THINGS THAT AREN'T HELPFUL DURING A MELTDOWN:

THESE ARE MY PREFERRED COMMUNICATION METHODS:

THINGS TO DO AFTER A MELTDOWN:

SENSORY SELF-SOOTHING

Sensory self-soothing is one of the most helpful distress tolerance skills in my opinion, especially for us neurodivergent folks with sensory differences.

Sensory self-soothing probably speaks for itself - the aim is to relieve any distress or overwhelm by soothing ourselves with our senses.

When we focus on our senses, we can provide feelings of comfort and even joy, reduce the intensity of the emotions we might be feeling and distract ourselves from any overwhelming thoughts and feelings.

Remember, everyone is different so take some time to figure out what works for you but here are some suggestions to get you started:

LOOK

go for a walk in nature
walk a feel-good movie
look at funny memes
watch TikTok videos

TASTE

sip on a cup of tea
bake cookies
focus on a hard candy

HEAR

listen to a calming playlist
listen an angry playlist
call a friend
listen to music as a distraction

SMELL

light a candle
bake cookies
keep a favourite scent on hand

TOUCH
have a shower or a bubble bath
cuddle your pet
use a weighted blanket

SENSORY SELF-SOOTHING

Self-soothing is all about soothing yourself with objects, smells or sounds that ground you and calm you. When you need it, you can come back to this list as a reminder or share it with your partner, family, parents or your doctor so they can also support you.

VISUAL

TASTE

SOUND

SMELL

TOUCH

IMPROVE THE ENVIRONMENT

You might have heard of the DBT skill, 'IMPROVE the Moment': a skill to help you tolerate emotions until they feel less intense by improving the moment in a variety of ways. Instead, we're going to focus on improving the environment.

Often our environment can contribute to sensory overload, meltdowns, distress and emotional overwhelm, which is why it's helpful to do what we can to make the changes in our current environment - especially if we can't simply remove ourselves.

The goal of this skill is to improve the environment in any way you can, to help you tolerate whatever emotions you might be feeling, until the intensity of the emotions reduces and to lower distress.

Remember, none of the tools to distract you are meant to invalidate or deny your current emotions - it's merely there to help you tolerate or distract yourself from powerful emotions until you're in a better space to deal with them more effectively.

IMAGE AND VISUAL:

Try dimming the lights, switching off overhead lights, or closing the curtains. You can also find a quiet room to retreat to or even curl up in a dark corner if you're comfortable.

Sometimes we need a distraction from our emotions, so putting on your comfort show, or favourite movie can give you time to calm down.

MOVEMENT AND STIMMING:

Stimming can help us to regulate and manage our emotions, sensations, or thoughts when they're feeling too much as well as help us avoid distress or a meltdown.

You can find a list of stims to try in this workbook on page 48.

ENCOURAGE BOUNDARIES:

One way to improve the environment is by encouraging or enforcing boundaries in the moment. For example, Ask someone to close the blinds and turn off lights.

PROPRIOCEPTIVE INPUT:

Deep pressure has been found to impact the part of the nervous system that regulates breathing, heart rate and more. Providing proprioceptive input like a weighted blanket or a weighted pillow can bring our systems to a more balanced state and help with distress.

REMOVE YOURSELF:

Sometimes it's the environment contributing to our distress and the best thing we can do, if it's possible, is take a break by removing yourself from the situation or environment.

OCCUPY ATTENTION WITH SPECIAL INTERESTS:

Special interests (see page 49) bring us joy, confidence and passion and are a source of well-being, coping and community which is why they should be utilised as a positive strategy in times of need.

Do you have a special interest or something you've been hyperfocusing on at the moment? Immerse yourself in your special interest.

VALIDATE:

Be kind to yourself and give yourself some hopeful encouragement. What do you need to hear to get through difficult times? Remind yourself that any emotions are temporary and that you've gotten through times like this in the past. Tell yourself that you've got this. Activate your inner cheerleader and talk to yourself through the crisis like you would if you were with a good friend.

A LIST OF STIMS

As neurodivergent individuals, stimming is an excellent way for us to regulate and self-soothe, but as we all know, we might be used to masking or haven't yet explored what it's like to stim. We also might need some reminders of ways to stim when we're experiencing distress and we can't think as clearly. This list can be a starting point.

- [ ] HAND FLAPPING/WAVING
- [ ] STIM DANCING
- [ ] TAPPING FEET/FINGERS
- [ ] TWIRLING YOUR HAIR
- [ ] SHAKING YOUR HEAD
- [ ] SINGING
- [ ] REPEATING WORDS
- [ ] MAKING SOUNDS
- [ ] RUBBING YOUR FACE OR FINGERS ON SOFT THINGS
- [ ] BITING THINGS OR USING CHEWELLERY
- [ ] USING BATH BOMBS

- [ ] ARM FLAPPING/WAVING
- [ ] LISTENING TO THE SAME SONG
- [ ] BOUNCING YOUR LEG
- [ ] BITING LIPS
- [ ] MOVING YOUR HANDS IN FRONT OF YOUR VISION
- [ ] WATCHING SOMETHING THAT'S REPETITIVE OR SOOTHING
- [ ] VISUAL STIMMING
- [ ] FIDGETING
- [ ] MIMICKING FACES/WORDS
- [ ] SEEKING PRESSURE FROM BLANKETS OR PETS
- [ ] SUCKING ON A MINT OR A LOLLIPOP

SPECIAL INTERESTS

Special interests (otherwise known as SpIns) are a source of well-being, coping and community and they can actually be used as a positive strategy as neurodivergent individuals. Engaging with our SpIns can help us distract ourselves as well as help us regulate and bring positive feelings.

SPINS THAT ARE AN ACTIVITY YOU CAN YOU DO

make up
cooking an baking
taking care of your plants
looking at the stars
arts and crafts
photography

_____

_____

_____

_____

SPINS YOU CAN LISTEN TO AND WATCH

TV shows
podcasts
music
YouTube videos

_____

_____

_____

_____

SPINS YOU CAN DEEP DIVE AND DISTRACT YOURSELF WITH

space and stars
plants
dinosaurs
neurodiversity

_____

_____

_____

_____

SPINS YOU CAN SHARE OR DO WITH OTHERS

doing make up
cooking or baking
arts and crafts
looking at photos

_____

_____

_____

_____

49

DISTRESS TOLERANCE SUMMARY

Which distress tolerance skills are most helpful for you?

What are some signs that you need to use these skills?

Can you identify any barriers or accommodations needed in using these skills?

What reminders do you need to use your distress tolerance skills?

SECTION 4:

EMOTIONAL REGULATION

52   The role of emotions

54   Emotional responses

55   Alexithymia

56   Describing your emotions

59   The Window of Tolerance

61   Emotional regulation

62   Check the facts

64   Act Intentionally

DOODLE HERE

THE ROLE OF EMOTIONS

Emotions aren't good or bad. They all serve a purpose, even if the emotion itself isn't entirely pleasant to feel. All emotions have a role to play and that role is communication: giving us information and bringing our attention to important things happening around us and to us.

COMMUNICATION

Emotions are a form of communication that allow us to communicate verbally and non-verbally with other people. Emotions also communicate with ourselves by providing us with information and input.

MOTIVATION

Emotions help to motivate and prepare us for action. Our emotions actually help activate and deactivate systems like perception, memory, attention, learning, and motivation. Cool, huh?

INFORMATION

Emotions give us information about a situation. Our emotions are necessary for survival which is why it's important we at least listen to them - it doesn't mean we have to always act on them though.

INFLUENCE OUR THOUGHTS

Our emotions are connected to our thoughts as well as our memories. Remember the movie *Inside Out*, and how spheres of memories were colour coded? It's kind of like that. It's why it's easier to think sad thoughts when we're sad or remember happy memories when we're happy.

EMOTIONS AS MESSENGERS

You now know that emotions serve an important role, providing us with information and helping us communicate. Our emotions are messengers but it might be helpful to understand how our emotions send us messengers and that's through the emotional triangle.

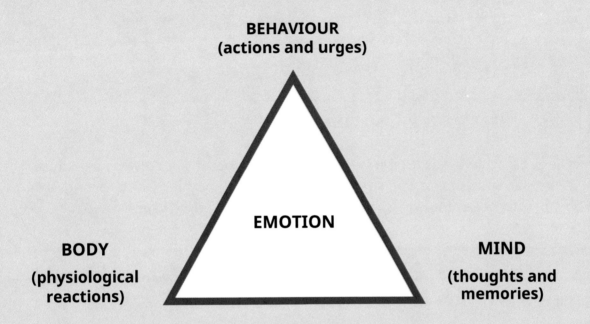

The emotional triangle refers to the three things that our emotions can impact; behaviour, physical responses and thoughts. When we start to become aware of these clues that our body, behaviour, and mind give us, it can be easier to identify and figure out the emotion we might be feeling. Remember, these emotions have important roles and they're trying to communicate with us.

If we consider our emotions to be a notification on our phone, if we keep ignoring the notification, it's going to keep beeping and telling us to pay attention to it. Well, our emotions are the same so these sensations, urges and thoughts usually get louder, harder to ignore and more difficult to manage. That's why recognising or identifying our emotions can be a helpful skill when learning to regulate them.

CHOOSE AN EMOTION TO FOCUS ON AND ASK YOURSELF:

- how does your body respond - what sensations do you notice?
- how does your mind respond - are your thoughts racing?
- how do you respond - what urge do you need to act upon?

EMOTIONAL RESPONSES

Our emotions are messengers and they can be useful in communicating things to us. However, sometimes our responses can be based on other factors that might not be helpful in the moment.

Emotions are complex and involve a whole-body response, so understanding how our emotional responses work can be empowering and helpful when it comes to identifying them and regulating them.

FIRST, THERE'S THE PROMPTING EVENT:

The prompting event triggers the first emotion, but it's not always an external event like someone saying something to you or something going wrong. It can be an internal event like your own thoughts, feeling tired or even sensory overload.

INTERPRETATION AND SECONDARY EMOTION

Often, our first emotion can trigger a second emotion in response, like feeling guilty after we've felt angry or feeling jealous when we feel insecure.
As we're all human, we often have an interpretation of the event that's influenced by so many things including our beliefs, RSD, and more.

PHYSICAL RESPONSES

As you know, our emotions are complex and involve a whole-body response, so there are always physical or body changes and responses going on with whatever emotion we're feeling. Our heart rate changes, our temperature changes, our breathing and more.

EXPRESSIONS

Our emotions and our physical responses impact our thoughts, words and behaviours like the things we say or want to say and actions we want to take, especially when it comes to intense emotions like anger, fear or anxiety.

ALEXITHYMIA

Alexithymia is a difference in emotional processing and a common experience in Autistic and ADHD individuals where we struggle identifying, describing and expressing our emotions. It can look like:

- having trouble finding the right words to describe what you're feeling
- difficulty expressing emotions using verbal words
- difficulty discriminating between emotions and bodily sensations
- difficulty in identifying faces and facial expressions

I'm someone who experiences alexithymia, and I like to describe it as lacking an internal label maker for emotions where I often have to rely on physical sensations to figure out what I'm feeling. This means I'll usually give vague approximations like "I'm fine" when someone asks how I am.

USE ALTERNATIVE DESCRIPTIONS

Try using alternative descriptions to describe your emotions or how you're feeling. One alternative is to describe physical sensations like "feeling tense" to describe anger or perhaps your stomach is feeling sore to describe anxiousness. Another alternative is to use activities to describe your emotions like "I just want to lie in bed all day" to describe sadness or "I want to throw something" to describe frustration.

EMOTION WHEEL

There are a number of emotion wheel charts available, which are helpful in identifying what emotion you might be feeling. Emotion wheels are helpful when you find it difficult to recognise and label an emotion especially if it's a complex emotion.

USE MUSIC OR LYRICS

You can also use music and lyrics to describe your emotions. I'm someone who often uses music and lyrics to both communicate and describe my emotions as well as a way to figure out my own emotions.

DESCRIBING YOUR EMOTIONS

When trying to identify or understand our emotions, breaking down our emotional experience can be really helpful. It also allows us to take a step back and see how we can meet our needs better and make any accommodations.

Emotions consist of the trigger (prompting event), any interpretations, beliefs or assumptions that you make, physiological changes or sensations in the body, and any urges or behaviours you might feel because of the emotion.

WHAT WAS THE PROMPTING EVENT?

Describe the prompting event. Remember it can be a combination of things or an external or internal event.

INTERPRETATIONS

Can you identify any thoughts or emotions you might have had in response? Are there any beliefs or past experiences that might have influenced this?

PHYSICAL RESPONSES

Noticing our physical responses and changes during emotional responses can be helpful in identifying our emotions as well as regulating them.

EXPRESSIONS

Notice the expressions like the actions or urges you might want to act upon or the words you want to say.

DESCRIBING YOUR EMOTIONS

Sometimes it can be hard to describe or identify our emotions, so I've included this section to make it a little easier. You will find a list of common emotions like anger or anxiety and with each emotion, a list of common sensations or things you might experience.

IF YOU'RE ANGRY, YOU MIGHT EXPERIENCE:

irritation
hurt
heart racing
hands clenching
feeling hot
inside is shaking
muscles tightening
mouth/jaw feel tight
a need to explode
like stomping or slamming

IF YOU'RE SAD, YOU MIGHT EXPERIENCE:

lonely
rejected
empty or hollow
a need to be alone
like crying
tired or fatigue
like you aren't interested
like you don't care

IF YOU'RE ANXIOUS, YOU MIGHT EXPERIENCE:

breathlessness
racing heart
fidgeting
frozen or tense
lump in throat
nausea
muscles tightening
overthinking
feeling clammy/cold

IF YOU'RE JEALOUS, YOU MIGHT EXPERIENCE:

rejection
insecure
racing heart
difficulty breathing
tight chest
feeling a need for control
racing thoughts
overthinking

DESCRIBING YOUR EMOTIONS

Everyone experiences emotions differently which means we might find we experience different sensations, thoughts or urges/behaviours. You can use this worksheet to describe how you personally experience certain emotions. Use the previous page for a starting point if you like.

**WHEN I'M _____
I MAY EXPERIENCE:**

**WHEN I'M _____
I MAY EXPERIENCE:**

**WHEN I'M _____
I MAY EXPERIENCE:**

**WHEN I'M _____
I MAY EXPERIENCE:**

WINDOW OF TOLERANCE

The Window of Tolerance was coined by Dr. Dan Siegel and it's since been adopted to understand our emotions. The zone of tolerance can be described as the perfect window where we aren't overstimulated or overwhelmed and we aren't understimulated or underwhelmed.

Everyone has their unique zone of tolerance where they can experience different emotions and remain within the zone or a regulated state. Here you can think clearly, process information and do what you need to do, so it's the ideal state to be in.

However, when emotions get too much (hyperarousal) or things are getting you down or you feel numb (hypoarousal), it can take you outside of that zone of tolerance and that's when things start happening e.g. anxiety, fast heart, racing thoughts vs disassociating, feeling numb or tired.

As neurodivergent individuals, we often feel emotions more easily and more intensely. While this can be a beautiful thing, experiencing intense joy and excitement over small things, it also means we experience the other, not so fun, emotions intensely too.

HYPERAROUSAL

flight or fight response	reactive emotions
anxiety and panic	shaking
fear	aggression
racing thoughts	defensiveness
inability to keep still	

ZONE OF TOLERANCE

feeling safe	regulating your emotions
feeling calm	insight and awareness
thinking clearly	being present in the moment
self-soothing	feeling all the emotions

HYPOAROUSAL

disassociation	numb
unable to think	withdrawn
intrusive thoughts	disconnected from self
no energy	shutting down
depression	fatigue

YOUR WINDOW OF TOLERANCE

Everyone has their unique zone of tolerance, so it can be helpful to understand what it looks like when we're in our zone and what it looks like when we're outside our zone. As emotions also influence our thoughts, physical sensations and our actions or urges, there's often a lot going on and a lot of signs to notice.

HYPERAROUSAL *Write down the signs or things you notice...*

↑

ZONE OF TOLERANCE *Write down the signs or things you notice...*

↓

HYPOAROUSAL *Write down the signs or things you notice...*

EMOTIONAL REGULATION

Emotional regulation is basically the ability to control and manage your emotions as well as your reactions to your emotions. This includes when you have them, how you experience them, and how you express or act on them. Emotional regulation is important because it keeps us within our optimal zone- our Window of Tolerance.

As neurodivergent individuals, emotional sensitivity and heightened emotions can make it harder to regulate our emotions. If you didn't have access to a safe environment or caregivers who were emotionally regulated, you might have trouble regulating your emotions because you didn't have an opportunity to learn. Emotional regulation isn't easy at all and there are a lot of factors that impact our ability to regulate including:

- executive function
- heightened emotions
- biological factors
- unlearned skills
- sensory processing
- masking
- alexithymia
- environment

If emotional regulation is the process of regulating and controlling our emotions, emotional dysregulation is the inability to regulate or control emotions, including our emotional experiences, actions and responses. It can look like:

- impulsiveness
- intense emotions
- acting on urges
- avoidance or attempts at numbing
- poor problem-solving
- fear of abandonment
- extreme emotional responses
- poor attempts at coping

Emotional regulation skills are helpful for everyone, especially for us neurodivergent individuals when we often experience big emotions, have difficulties with executive function and regulating our emotions.

That's where these DBT skills come in handy! These skills focus on emotional regulation and can help shift you back to that zone of tolerance where you function best. Just like every kind of skill, it takes practice and figuring out what works best for you.

CHECK THE FACTS
IS IT HELPFUL?

While our emotions are always valid, our responses to our emotions sometimes need double-checking before we act on them or allow them to steer us.

We don't want to focus on whether our emotions fit the facts though. We want to focus on whether our response to our emotions (the desired action or behaviour) fits the facts and whether responding in this way is helpful to us in the moment.

This is because our responses can sometimes be set off by how we interpret or think about an event/situation rather than the event itself. They can also be impacted by our previous experiences, beliefs, and sometimes, just poor emotional regulation and impulsivity.

And that's okay - this is where checking the facts comes in handy.

When we examine our emotions and explore our responses and the facts of the event, we can determine whether our responses are helpful. If they aren't helpful, we can use checking the facts to become aware and figure out what would be helpful.

Remember, before we check the facts, we should always also always check our needs because often, our emotions are communicating a need and we need to learn to listen.

You can start by using these prompts below:

> Identify your emotion and your response to your emotion. This can be something you want to act upon like if you're angry, you may want to scream or throw something.

> Identify your interpretations, thoughts, assumptions and beliefs about the event or situation.

> Is your response to your emotion helpful to you? Will your response meet your needs? Ask yourself if acting on the emotion is effective - sometimes it is!

CHECK IF IT'S HELPFUL

**DOES MY RESPONSE
FIT THE FACTS?**

YES

NO

IS IT HELPFUL?

IS IT HELPFUL?

YES

YES

**HOW CAN I REGULATE
MY EMOTIONS?**

Proceed mindfully and do
your thing

_____

_____

**HOW CAN I REGULATE
MY EMOTIONS?**

Act intentionally

Use emotional
regulation skills

_____

NO

NO

**WHAT CAN I
DO INSTEAD?**

Use distress
tolerance skills

Act intentionally

_____

**WHAT CAN I
DO INSTEAD?**

Use distress
tolerance skills

Repeat affirmations

Challenge thoughts

ACT INTENTIONALLY

You might have heard of the DBT skill "Act Opposite" which is a skill to help you manage your emotions by responding in an opposite way. As a neurodivergent individual, I've always struggled with this skill because I struggle to figure out what the opposite is and for me, acting opposite isn't always helpful and it often feels invalidating.

That's why I've renamed it to "Act Intentionally" because this skill is about exploring how to respond intentionally to your emotions.

Remember how our emotions are important messengers and they often come with an urge or behaviour that we might want to act on? If you're feeling sad, you might feel the need to isolate yourself or cry. If you're feeling anger, you might feel the need to scream or throw something.

Often our urges following our emotions will make sense for the situation we're in, especially when it's a survival response (like running when we experience fear), but sometimes our emotional response might not always fit the facts of the situation.

This is where we would act intentionally and perhaps pick the opposite of the urge like walking away when we're angry instead of throwing something when it's not appropriate or reaching out for company instead of isolating.

Sometimes it really does help to throw a soft toy or scream into a pillow though.

WHEN YOU'RE ANGRY OR FRUSTRATED

Tear up magazines
Scream loudly to music
Dance furiously around the room
Jump on a trampoline
Throw balled up socks
Draw, paint or throw paint
Scrunch up pieces of paper
Build something then destroy it
Ask a friend if you can vent

_____

_____

WHEN YOU'RE FEELING LONELY OR SAD:

Look at photos
Remember funny conversations
Ask someone over for a visit
Call a warmline
Watch a favourite show or movie
Eat a favourite or safe food
Watch funny videos or tiktoks
Hug a pet
Draw or paint with your sadness

_____

_____

ACT INTENTIONALLY

WHEN YOU'RE FEELING SCARED OR ANXIOUS:

Wrap yourself in a blanket

Listen to music

Write down a list of reality checks

Use your senses for grounding

Use the TIPP skill

Solve a puzzle or play a game

_____

_____

_____

WHEN YOU'RE FEELING

_____

WHEN YOU'RE FEELING

_____

WHEN YOU'RE FEELING

_____

EMOTIONAL REGULATION SUMMARY

What emotional regulation skills/tools are most helpful for you?

```


```

What are some that signs you need to use these skills?

```


```

Can you identify any barriers or accommodations needed in using these skills?

```


```

What reminders do you need to use these skills and tools?

```


```

SECTION 5:

MANAGING SENSORY NEEDS

68   Sensory profile and needs

69   Hypersensitivity

71   Hyposensitivity

73   Sensory overload

74   My sensory profile

76   Build a sensory toolkit

DOODLE HERE

SENSORY PROFILE & NEEDS

It's a natural human experience to have our own sensory profile, and by that I mean our own unique sensory processing system and needs. However, as neurodivergent individuals, we're often more likely to have a different sensory processing system. Our sensory processing system takes in information we receive from all our senses and processes them so we can respond accordingly.

You might've heard of the five senses, but we actually have eight senses that impact our sensory needs and differences! Our external senses are the five senses we know; **sight, touch, smell, taste** and **sound.** We also have three internal senses which are **vestibular, proprioception** and **interoception**.

Proprioception is our body awareness and spatial awareness while our interoception is our internal body awareness like hunger cues. The third internal sense is vestibular, which is related to our balance and why you might experience motion sickness - because your vestibular system is over-sensitive!

Everyone manages and receives sensory input differently so our needs are unique and our sensory needs can shift as our environment changes and our capacity shifts.

A way to understand our sensory differences or sensitivities is by looking at our preferences with hypersensitivity and hyposensitivity. Everyone can experience both hyper and hyposensitivity with one, some, or many of the senses and our preferences can change daily, weekly or depending on different things.

Hypersensitivity

Hypersensitivity is an over-responsiveness to sensory input that can cause sensory overload, distress, discomfort and pain. Individuals who are hypersensitive tend to avoid certain stimuli or sensory input or need frequent breaks from sensory input.

Hyposensitivity

Hyposensitivity is an under-responsiveness to sensory input where individuals often struggle to register low levels of sensory input or may receive less information from the senses. Individuals who are hyposensitive tend to seek out and need higher levels of sensory input and stimulation.

EXAMPLES OF HYPERSENSITIVITY

VISUAL

- sensitive to light especially when sleeping
- details are easier to focus on
- lights appear too bright

SMELL

- sensitive to smells
- perfumes and shampoos are overpowering
- refusal to eat certain foods

SOUND

- sensitive to background noises
- multiple sounds are overwhelming
- startled by loud noises

TASTE

- certain textures cause discomfort and distress
- predictable diet and safe foods
- flavours are overwhelming

PROPRIOCEPTION

- prefer to sit down or remain grounded
- often leaning
- difficulties with fine motor skills

TOUCH

- hair brushing can cause discomfort
- textures on skin are irritating
- difficulty with wet textures

VESTIBULAR

- often gets car and motion sickness
- avoids swings, ladders, merry go rounds
- loses balance easily

INTEROCEPTION

- easily overwhelmed by internal sensations
- heightened sensitivity to physiological cues
- can cause anxiety or discomfort

MANAGING HYPERSENSITIVITY

VISUAL

- reduce fluorescent lighting
- utilise lamps
- use sunglasses
- reduce clutter/visual distractions

SMELL

- use fragrance free products
- ask for events or parties to be perfume free
- keep rooms ventilated

SOUND

- use noise cancelling headphones
- try out earplugs
- have a quiet area away from background noises

TASTE

- eat your preferred food
- don't force yourself to eat foods you don't want
- use chewellery (chew jewellery)

PROPRIOCEPTION

- reduce items with buttons/ laces
- use different seating like bean bags
- use grippy tools for items like pens or keys

TOUCH

- remove tags from clothing
- use seamless socks and items
- ask for firmer pressure over lighter pressure

VESTIBULAR

- reduce car ride length
- sit in front to reduce motion sickness
- regular breaks from movement activities

INTEROCEPTION

- use visual prompts and communication scripts
- frequent self-care breaks
- regulation strategies

EXAMPLES OF HYPOSENSITIVITY

VISUAL

- poor depth perception
- trouble locating an item
- difficulty identifying differences in pictures, words, etc

SMELL

- difficulty interpreting smells
- enjoys foods with strong smells
- uses smell to engage with objects or people

SOUND

- attracted to loud spaces
- difficulty localizing a sound
- often turns music or the TV up louder to register

TASTE

- likes foods with intense flavours
- has a predictable diet
- big on tactile stimming
- putting items in mouth

PROPRIOCEPTION

- difficulty navigating a room
- crashes into furniture
- prefers tight clothing and heavy blankets
- trouble balancing

TOUCH

- high pain threshold
- likes tight clothing and weighted blankets
- requires tight hugs to register the pressure

VESTIBULAR

- seeks all forms of movement like swinging
- frequent rocking back and forth
- always seeking stimuli

INTEROCEPTION

- difficulty sensing when hungry or thirsty
- requires more input to sense
- trouble interpreting what we're feeling

MANAGING HYPOSENSITIVITY

VISUAL

- have items on open shelves so it's easier to find
- have multiple forms of lighting
- reduce clutter

SMELL

- have scented items on hand
- CLEARLY label foods and items

SOUND

- provide visual cues & instructions
- ask for instructions to be broken down
- listen to music for sensory input

TASTE

- wear chew jewellery
- list of safe or same foods
- crunchy snacks on hand

PROPRIOCEPTION

- keep a room clear from furniture
- use input like weighted blankets
- use grip pens/weighted pens

TOUCH

- provide lots of fidget items
- use weighted blankets
- ask friends/partners for tighter hugs and pressure

VESTIBULAR

- get a chair swing, exercise ball or mini trampoline at home
- introduce a sensory diet
- frequent movement breaks

INTEROCEPTION

- regular check ins/breaks
- alternative descriptions
- accessible hydration options
- simple, quick snacks

SENSORY OVERLOAD

Neurodivergent individuals process sensory information differently every day. We may be hypersensitive or hyposensitive, or even both, at different times. Our sensory differences can impact how we feel, how we cope and can have a significant impact on our lives. As we live in a society that is full of sensory input that doesn't necessarily accommodate our needs, we can end up overstimulated from our environments.

Sensory overload is what happens when we receive too much input from our senses. These senses are the five senses we know; visual, touch, smell, taste and sound as well as the three internal senses which are; vestibular, proprioception and interoception.

When some or even all of these senses receive too much input for our brain to process and handle, we become overwhelmed which can cause a lot of discomfort, pain and distress. Our sensory differences can also impact our functioning and our everyday lives, from emotional regulation to getting things done to socialising.

It's normal and common for every human to have limits on the amount of sensory input we need and can handle, but for neurodivergent individuals, our brains receive and process sensory input differently, which means we're more likely to reach our limits and experience sensory overload.

Signs of Sensory Overload

irritability	difficulty focusing
restlessness	feeling wound up
fidgeting	headaches
increased stimming	freeze response
need to escape or avoid	feeling instantly exhausted
everything is moving too fast	

The best way to respond to sensory overload is by reducing or removing the sensory input that is contributing to the sensory overload. In order to do this, you need to have an understanding of your sensory needs and differences.

You can do this by filling in the sensory profile worksheets in the following pages and exploring ways to manage your sensory differences.

MY SENSORY PROFILE

FILL IN THE LEVEL OF
HYPERSENSITIVITY YOU
EXPERIENCE WITH EACH
OF THE SENSES:

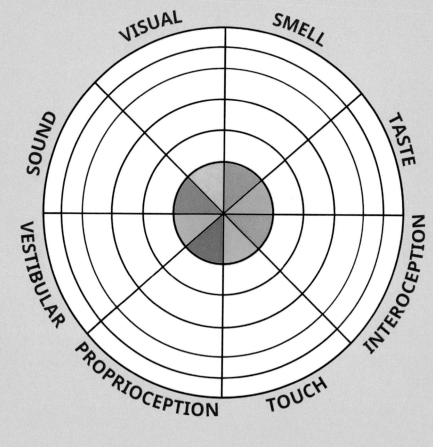

1 - no impact on my quality of life
2 - occasionally but minimal impact
3 - sometimes but easy to manage
4 - regularly interferes
5 - uses up all my spoons

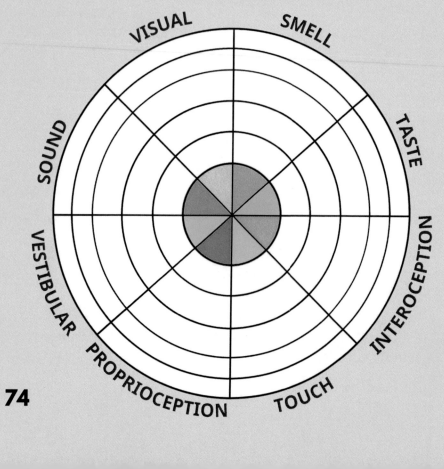

FILL IN THE LEVEL OF
HYPOSENSITIVITY YOU
EXPERIENCE WITH EACH
OF THE SENSES:

1 - no impact on my quality of life
2 - occasionally but minimal impact
3 - sometimes but easy to manage
4 - regularly interferes
5 - uses up all my spoons

MY SENSORY PROFILE

You can use this worksheet to list your particular sensory differences and needs including hypersensitivities and hyposensitivites.

VISUAL

SMELL

SOUND

TASTE

PROPRIOCEPTION

(external body awareness)

TOUCH

VESTIBULAR

(sense of balance/movement)

INTEROCEPTION

(what's going on inside your body)

BUILD A SENSORY TOOLKIT

A sensory toolkit is something designed to help soothe and comfort you during times of distress or sensory overload.

Some tips to get you started:

Everyone is different, so ask yourself, "do I find this sensation pleasant or unpleasant? Comforting or uncomfortable?"

You might find you need different types of sensory items depending on the day and your sensory needs.

Keep the toolkit somewhere accessible because the idea is that you or anyone you live with can easily pull it out whenever you need it.

Consider keeping a set of instructions in the toolkit for your partner, loved one or even yourself.

VISUAL

ambient lighting like fairy lights
affirmation cards
kaleidoscope
glitter jar
light-up toys
bubbles

SOUNDS

noise-cancelling headphones
playlist with nature sounds
sound of your cat purring
white noise machine
audiobook

TOUCH

favourite soft toy
weighted blanket
play dough, slime
stress balls
wooden puzzles
bubble wrap

SMELL

play-dough with a favourite scent
scented lotion
scented pillow
calming spray
scratch and sniff stickers

BUILD YOUR OWN SENSORY TOOLKIT

VISUAL

experiment with objects that are visually mesmerising or calming.

SOUNDS

what you might need may change depending on the day.

TOUCH

experiment with different textures and things to keep your hands busy

SMELL

do you have any smells associated with positive memories?

Made in the USA
Middletown, DE
21 August 2024

59587697R00044